Peter Constandy

SUDDENLY LAST SUMMER

By TENNESSEE WILLIAMS

PLAYS

Baby Doll (a screenplay)
Camino Real
Cat on a Hot Tin Roof
The Glass Menagerie
Orpheus Descending (with Battle of Angels)
The Rose Tattoo
A Streetcar Named Desire
Suddenly Last Summer
Summer and Smoke
Sweet Bird of Youth
27 Wagons Full of Cotton and Other Plays
You Touched Me (with Donald Windham)

POETRY

Five Young American Poets, 1944
In the Winter of Cities

PROSE

Hard Candy and Other Stories
One Arm and Other Stories
The Roman Spring of Mrs. Stone

Hortense Alden as Mrs. Venable, Robert Lansing as
Dr. Cukrowicz and Anne Meacham as Catherine Holly
in SUDDENLY LAST SUMMER. *Photo by Friedman-Abeles*

SUDDENLY LAST SUMMER

by TENNESSEE WILLIAMS

A NEW DIRECTIONS BOOK

Library of Congress Catalog Card Number: 58-9512

SECOND PRINTING

Book Design by Stefan Salter

Manufactured in the United States of America
New Directions Books are published by James Laughlin
New York Office—333 Sixth Avenue

To Anne Meacham

Suddenly Last Summer, with *Something Unspoken,* were presented together under the collective title of *Garden District* at the York Theatre on First Avenue in New York on January 7, 1958 by John C. Wilson and Warner Le Roy. It was directed by Herbert Machiz; the stage set was designed by Robert Soule and the costumes by Stanley Simmons. Lighting was by Lee Watson and the incidental music was by Ned Rorem. *Something Unspoken* was published in the latest edition of *27 Wagons Full of Cotton and Other Plays.*

CAST OF CHARACTERS

MRS. VENABLE	HORTENSE ALDEN
DR. CUKROWICZ	ROBERT LANSING
MISS FOXHILL	DONNA CAMERON
MRS. HOLLY	ELEANOR PHELPS
GEORGE HOLLY	ALAN MIXON
CATHARINE HOLLY	ANNE MEACHAM
SISTER FELICITY	NANON-KIAM

SUDDENLY LAST SUMMER

SCENE ONE

The set may be as unrealistic as the decor of a dramatic ballet. It represents part of a mansion of Victorian Gothic style in the Garden District of New Orleans on a late afternoon, between late summer and early fall. The interior is blended with a fantastic garden which is more like a tropical jungle, or forest, in the prehistoric age of giant fern-forests when living creatures had flippers turning to limbs and scales to skin. The colors of this jungle-garden are violent, especially since it is steaming with heat after rain. There are massive tree-flowers that suggest organs of a body, torn out, still glistening with undried blood; there are harsh cries and sibilant hissings and thrashing sounds in the garden as if it were inhabited by beasts, serpents and birds, all of savage nature. . . .

The jungle tumult continues a few moments after the curtain rises; then subsides into relative quiet, which is occasionally broken by a new outburst.

A lady enters with the assistance of a silver-knobbed cane. She

*has light orange or pink hair and wears a lavender lace dress,
and over her withered bosom is pinned a starfish of diamonds.*

*She is followed by a young blond Doctor, all in white, glacially
brilliant, very, very good-looking, and the old lady's manner
and eloquence indicate her undeliberate response to his icy
charm.*

MRS. VENABLE:
Yes, this was Sebastian's garden. The Latin names of the
plants were printed on tags attached to them but the print's
fading out. Those ones there—[*She draws a deep breath*]—
are the oldest plants on earth, survivors from the age of the
giant fern-forests. Of course in this semitropical climate—
[*She takes another deep breath*]—some of the rarest plants,
such as the Venus flytrap—you know what this is, Doctor?
The Venus flytrap?

DOCTOR:
An insectivorous plant?

MRS. VENABLE:
Yes, it feeds on insects. It has to be kept under glass from
early fall to late spring and when it went under glass, my son,
Sebastian, had to provide it with fruit flies flown in at great
expense from a Florida laboratory that used fruit flies for
experiments in genetics. Well, I can't do that, Doctor. [*She
takes a deep breath.*] I can't, I just can't do it! It's not the
expense but the—

DOCTOR:
Effort.

MRS. VENABLE:
Yes. So goodbye, Venus flytrap!—like so much else . . . Whew!
. . . [*She draws breath.*]—I don't know why, but—! I already
feel I can lean on your shoulder, Doctor—Cu?—Cu?

14

DOCTOR:

Cu-kro-wicz. It's a Polish word that means sugar, so let's make it simple and call me Doctor Sugar.

[*He returns her smile.*]

MRS. VENABLE:

Well, now, Doctor Sugar, you've seen Sebastian's garden.

[*They are advancing slowly to the patio area.*]

DOCTOR:

It's like a well-groomed jungle. . . .

MRS. VENABLE:

That's how he meant it to be, nothing was accidental, everything was planned and designed in Sebastian's life and his— [*She dabs her forehead with her handkerchief which she had taken from her reticule*]—work!

DOCTOR:

What was your son's work, Mrs. Venable?—besides this garden?

MRS. VENABLE:

As many times as I've had to answer that question! D'you know it still shocks me a little?—to realize that Sebastian Venable the poet is still unknown outside of a small coterie of friends, including his mother.

DOCTOR:

Oh.

MRS. VENABLE:

You see, strictly speaking, his *life* was his occupation.

DOCTOR:

I see.

MRS. VENABLE:

No, you *don't* see, yet, but before I'm through, you will.—

15

Sebastian was a poet! That's what I meant when I said his life was his work because the work of a poet is the life of a poet and—vice versa, the life of a poet is the work of a poet, I mean you can't separate them, I mean—well, for instance, a salesman's work is one thing and his life is another—or can be. The same thing's true of—doctor, lawyer, merchant, *thief*! —But a poet's life is his work and his work is his life in a special sense because—oh, I've already talked myself breathless and dizzy.

[*The Doctor offers his arm.*]

Thank you.

DOCTOR:

Mrs. Venable, did your doctor okay this thing?

MRS. VENABLE [*breathless*]:

What thing?

DOCTOR:

Your meeting this girl that you think is responsible for your son's death?

MRS. VENABLE:

I've waited months to face her because I couldn't get to St. Mary's to face her—I've had her brought here to my house. I won't collapse! She'll collapse! I mean her lies will collapse —not my truth—not the truth. . . . *Forward march, Doctor Sugar!*

[*He conducts her slowly to the patio.*]

Ah, we've *made* it, *ha ha*! I didn't know that I was so weak on my pins! Sit down, Doctor. I'm not afraid of using every last ounce and inch of my little, left-over strength in doing just what I'm doing. I'm devoting all that's left of my life, Doctor, to the defense of a dead poet's reputation. Sebastian had no public name as a poet, he didn't want one, he refused

16

to have one. He *dreaded, abhorred*!—false values that come
from being publicly known, from fame, from personal—
exploitation. . . . Oh, he'd say to me: "Violet? Mother?—
You're going to outlive me!!"

DOCTOR:
What made him think that?

MRS. VENABLE:
Poets are always clairvoyant!—And he had rheumatic fever
when he was fifteen and it affected a heart-valve and he
wouldn't stay off horses and out of water and so forth. . . .
"Violet? Mother? You're going to live longer than me, and
then, when I'm gone, it will be yours, in your hands, to do
whatever you please with!"—Meaning, of course, his future
recognition!—That he *did* want, he wanted it after his death
when it couldn't disturb him; then he did want to offer his
work to the world. All right. Have I made my point, Doctor?
Well, here is my son's work, Doctor, here's his life going *on*!

[*She lifts a thin gilt-edged volume from the patio table as
if elevating the Host before the altar. Its gold leaf and
lettering catch the afternoon sun. It says* Poem of Summer.
*Her face suddenly has a different look, the look of a
visionary, an exalted* religieuse. *At the same instant a bird
sings clearly and purely in the garden and the old lady
seems to be almost young for a moment.*]

DOCTOR [*reading the title*]:
Poem of Summer?

MRS. VENABLE:
Poem of Summer, and the date of the summer, there are
twenty-five of them, he wrote one poem a year which he
printed himself on an eighteenth-century hand-press at his—
atelier in the—French—Quarter—so no one but he could
see it. . . .

17

[*She seems dizzy for a moment.*]

DOCTOR:

He wrote one poem a year?

MRS. VENABLE:

One for each summer that we traveled together. The other nine months of the year were really only a preparation.

DOCTOR:

Nine months?

MRS. VENABLE:

The length of a pregnancy, yes. . . .

DOCTOR:

The poem was hard to deliver?

MRS. VENABLE:

Yes, even with me! *Without* me, *impossible*, Doctor!—he wrote no poem last summer.

DOCTOR:

He died last summer?

MRS. VENABLE:

Without me he died last summer, that was his last summer's poem.

[*She staggers; he assists her toward a chair. She catches her breath with difficulty.*]

One long-ago summer—now, why am I thinking of this?— my son, Sebastian, said, "Mother?—Listen to this!"—He read me Herman Melville's description of the Encantadas, the Galapagos Islands. Quote—take five and twenty heaps of cinders dumped here and there in an outside city lot. Imagine some of them magnified into mountains, and the vacant lot, the sea. And you'll have a fit idea of the general aspect of the Encantadas, the Enchanted Isles—extinct volcanos, looking

18

much as the world at large might look—after a last con-
flagration—end quote. He read me that description and said
that we had to go there. And so we did go there that summer
on a chartered boat, a four-masted schooner, as close as possible to the sort of a boat that Melville must have sailed
on. . . . We saw the Encantadas, but on the Encantadas we
saw something Melville *hadn't* written about. We saw the
great sea-turtles crawl up out of the sea for their annual
egg-laying. . . . Once a year the female of the sea-turtle crawls
up out of the equatorial sea onto the blazing sand-beach of a
volcanic island to dig a pit in the sand and deposit her eggs
there. It's a long and dreadful thing, the depositing of the eggs
in the sand-pits, and when it's finished the exhausted female
turtle crawls back to the sea half-dead. She never sees her
offspring, but we did. Sebastian knew exactly when the sea-
turtle eggs would be hatched out and we returned in time for
it. . . .

DOCTOR:
You went back to the—?

MRS. VENABLE:
Terrible Encantadas, those heaps of extinct volcanos, in time
to witness the hatching of the sea-turtles and their desperate
flight to the sea!

[*There is a sound of harsh bird-cries in the air. She looks
up.*]

—The narrow beach, the color of caviar, was all in motion!
But the sky was in motion, too. . . .

DOCTOR:
The sky was in motion, too?

MRS. VENABLE:
—Full of flesh-eating birds and the noise of the birds, the
horrible savage cries of the—

19

DOCTOR:

Carnivorous birds?

MRS. VENABLE:

Over the narrow black beach of the Encantadas as the just hatched sea-turtles scrambled out of the sand-pits and started their race to the sea. . . .

DOCTOR:

Race to the sea?

MRS. VENABLE:

To escape the flesh-eating birds that made the sky almost as black as the beach!

[*She gazes up again: we hear the wild, ravenous, harsh cries of the birds. The sound comes in rhythmic waves like a savage chant.*]

And the sand all alive, all alive, as the hatched sea-turtles made their dash for the sea, while the birds hovered and swooped to attack and hovered and—swooped to attack! They were diving down on the hatched sea-turtles, turning them over to expose their soft undersides, tearing the undersides open and rending and eating their flesh. Sebastian guessed that possibly only a hundredth of one per cent of their number would escape to the sea. . . .

DOCTOR:

What was it about this spectacle on the beach that fascinated your son?

MRS. VENABLE:

My son was looking for—

[*Stops short: continues evasively—*]

Let's just say he was interested in sea-turtles.

DOCTOR:

You started to say that your son was looking for something.

MRS. VENABLE:

[*defiantly*]

All right, I started to say that my son was looking for God and I stopped myself because I was afraid that if I said he was looking for God, you'd say to yourself, 'Oh, a pretentious young crack-pot!'—which Sebastian was not. All poets look for God, all good poets do, and they have to look harder for Him than priests do since they don't have the help of such famous guide-books and well-organized expeditions as priests have with their scriptures and churches. All right! Well, now I've said it, my son was looking for God. I mean for a clear image of Him. He spent that whole blazing equatorial day in the crow's nest of the schooner watching that thing on the beach of the Endantadas till it was too dark to see it, and when he came back down the rigging, he said, Well, now I've seen Him!—and he meant God . . .

DOCTOR:

I see.

MRS. VENABLE:

For several days after that he had a fever, he was delirious with it. I took command of the ship and we sailed North by East into cooler waters . . .

[*Miss Foxhill comes out silently on rubber-soled white oxfords, and waits to be noticed. She carries a water glass.*]

Next? India, China!—In the Himalayas—

[*Notices Miss Foxhill*]

What? Oh, elixir of—ha!—Isn't it kind of the drugstore to keep me alive!

[*Tosses down medicine with a wry face and dismisses Miss Foxhill with a slight gesture.*]

Where was I?

21

DOCTOR:
In the Himalayas.

MRS. VENABLE:
Oh yes, that long-ago summer. . . . In the Himalayas he almost
entered a Buddhist monastery, had gone so far as to shave his
head and eat just rice out of a wood bowl on a grass mat.
He'd promised those sly Buddhist monks that he would give
up the world and himself and all his worldly possessions to
their mendicant order.—Well, I cabled his father, "For God's
sake notify bank to freeze Sebastian's accounts!"—I got back
this cable from my late husband's lawyer: "Mr. Venable
critically ill Stop Wants you Stop Needs you Stop Immediate
return advised most strongly. Stop. Cable time of arrival. . . ."

DOCTOR:
Did you go back to your husband?

MRS. VENABLE:
I made the hardest decision of my life. I stayed with my son.
I got him through that crisis too. In less than a month he got
up off the filthy grass mat and threw the rice bowl away—
and booked us into Shepheard's Hotel in Cairo and the Ritz
in Paris—. And from then on, oh, we—still lived in a—world
of light and shadow. . . .

[*She turns vaguely with empty glass. He rises and takes it
from her.*]

But the shadow was almost as luminous as the light.

DOCTOR:
Don't you want to sit down now?

MRS. VENABLE:
Yes, indeed I do, before I fall down.

[*He assists her into wheelchair.*]

—Are your hind-legs still on you?

DOCTOR [*still concerned over her agitation*]:
—My what? Oh—hind legs!—Yes . . .

MRS. VENABLE:
Well, then you're not a donkey, you're certainly not a donkey because I've been talking the hind-legs off a donkey—several donkeys. . . . But I had to make it clear to you that the world lost a great deal too when I lost my son last summer. . . . You would have liked my son, he would have been charmed by you. My son, Sebastian, was not a family snob or a money snob but he was a snob, all right. He was a snob about personal charm in people, he insisted upon good looks in people around him, and, oh, he had a perfect little court of young and beautiful people around him always, wherever he was, here in New *Orleans* or New York or on the Riviera or in Paris and Venice, he always had a little entourage of the beautiful and the talented and the young!

DOCTOR:
Your son was young, Mrs. Venable?

MRS. VENABLE:
Both of us were young, and stayed young, Doctor.

DOCTOR:
Could I see a photograph of your son, Mrs. Venable?

MRS. VENABLE:
Yes, indeed you could, Doctor. I'm glad that you asked to see one. I'm going to show you not one photograph but two. Here. Here is my son, Sebastian, in a Renaissance pageboy's costume at a masked ball in Cannes. Here is my son, Sebastian, in the same costume at a masked ball in Venice. These two pictures were taken twenty years apart. Now which is the older one, Doctor?

DOCTOR:
This photograph looks older.

23

MRS. VENABLE:

The photograph looks older but not the subject. It takes character to refuse to grow old, Doctor—successfully to refuse to. It calls for discipline, abstention. One cocktail before dinner, not two, four, six—a single lean chop and lime juice on a salad in restaurants famed for rich dishes.

[*Foxhill comes from the house.*]

FOXHILL:

Mrs. Venable, Miss Holly's mother and brother are—

[*Simultaneously Mrs. Holly and George appear in the window.*]

GEORGE:

Hi, Aunt Vi!

MRS. HOLLY:

Violet dear, we're here.

FOXHILL:

They're here.

MRS. VENABLE:

Wait upstairs in my upstairs living room for me.

[*To Miss Foxhill:*]

Get them upstairs. I don't want them at that window during this talk.

[*To the Doctor:*]

Let's get away from the window.

[*He wheels her to stage center.*]

DOCTOR:

Mrs. Venable? Did your son have a—well—what kind of a *personal*, well, *private* life did—

MRS. VENABLE:

That's a question I wanted you to ask me.

DOCTOR:

Why?

MRS. VENABLE:

I haven't heard the girl's story except indirectly in a watered-down version, being too ill to go to hear it directly, but I've gathered enough to know that it's a hideous attack on my son's moral character which, being dead, he can't defend himself from. I have to be the defender. Now. Sit down. Listen to me . . .

[*The Doctor sits.*]

. . . before you hear whatever you're going to hear from the girl when she gets here. My son, Sebastian, was chaste. Not c-h-a-s-e-d! Oh, he was chased in that way of spelling it, too, we had to be very fleet-footed I can tell you, with his looks and his charm, to keep ahead of pursuers, every kind of pursuer!—I mean he was c-h-a-s-t-e!—Chaste. . . .

DOCTOR:

I understood what you meant, Mrs. Venable.

MRS. VENABLE:

And you *believe* me, don't you?

DOCTOR:

Yes, but—

MRS. VENABLE:

But *what*?

DOCTOR:

Chastity at—what age was your son last summer?

MRS. VENABLE:

Forty, maybe. We really didn't count birthdays. . . .

25

DOCTOR:
He lived a celibate life?

MRS. VENABLE:
As strictly as if he'd *vowed* to! This sounds like vanity, Doctor, but really I was actually the only one in his life that satisfied the demands he made of people. Time after time my son would let people go, dismiss them!—because their, their, their!—*attitude* toward him was—

DOCTOR:
Not as pure as—

MRS. VENABLE:
My son, Sebastian, demanded! We were a famous couple. People didn't speak of Sebastian and his mother or Mrs. Venable and her son, they said "Sebastian and Violet, Violet and Sebastian are staying at the Lido, they're at the Ritz in Madrid. Sebastian and Violet, Violet and Sebastian have taken a house at Biarritz for the season," and every appearance, every time we appeared, attention was centered on *us*! —*everyone else*! *Eclipsed*! Vanity? Ohhhh, no, Doctor, you can't call it that—

DOCTOR:
I didn't call it that.

MRS. VENABLE:
—It wasn't *folie de grandeur*, it was grandeur.

DOCTOR:
I see.

MRS. VENABLE:
An attitude toward life that's hardly been known in the world since the great Renaissance princes were crowded out of their palaces and gardens by successful shopkeepers!

26

DOCTOR:
I see.

MRS. VENABLE:
Most people's lives—what are they but trails of debris, each day more debris, more debris, long, long trails of debris with nothing to clean it all up but, finally, death. . . .

[*We hear lyric music.*]

My son, Sebastian, and I constructed our days, each day, we would—carve out each day of our lives like a piece of sculpture.—Yes, we left behind us a trail of days like a gallery of sculpture! But, last summer—

[*Pause: the music continues.*]

I can't forgive him for it, not even now that he's paid for it with his life!—he let in this—*vandal*! This—

DOCTOR:
The girl that—?

MRS. VENABLE:
That you're going to meet here this afternoon! Yes. He admitted this vandal and with her tongue for a hatchet she's gone about smashing our legend, the memory of—

DOCTOR:
Mrs. Venable, what do you think is her reason?

MRS. VENABLE:
Lunatics don't have reason!

DOCTOR:
I mean what do you think is her—motive?

MRS. VENABLE:
What a question!—We put the bread in her mouth and the clothes on her back. People that like you for that or even forgive you for it are, are—*hen's teeth,* Doctor. The role of

27

the benefactor is worse than thankless, it's the role of a victim, Doctor, a sacrificial victim, yes, they want your blood, Doctor, they want your blood on the altar steps of their *outraged, outrageous* egos!

DOCTOR:
Oh. You mean she resented the—

MRS. VENABLE:
Loathed!—They can't shut her up at St. Mary's.

DOCTOR:
I thought she'd been there for months.

MRS. VENABLE:
I mean keep her *still* there. She *babbles*! They couldn't shut her up in Cabeza de Lobo or at the clinic in Paris—she babbled, babbled!—smashing my son's reputation.—On the Berengaria bringing her back to the States she broke out of the stateroom and babbled, babbled; even at the airport when she was flown down here, she babbled a bit of her story before they could whisk her into an ambulance to St. Mary's. This is a reticule, Doctor. [*She raises a cloth bag.*] A catch-all, carry-all bag for an elderly lady which I turned into last summer. . . . Will you open it for me, my hands are stiff, and fish out some cigarettes and a cigarette holder.

[*He does.*]

DOCTOR:
I don't have matches.

MRS. VENABLE:
I think there's a table-lighter on the table.

DOCTOR:
Yes, there is,

[*He lights it, it flames up high.*]

My Lord, what a torch!

28

MRS. VENABLE [*with a sudden, sweet smile*]:
"So shines a good deed in a naughty world," Doctor—
Sugar. . . .

[*Pause. A bird sings sweetly in the garden.*]

DOCTOR:
Mrs. Venable?

MRS. VENABLE:
Yes?

DOCTOR:
In your letter last week you made some reference to a, to a—
fund of some kind, an endowment fund of—

MRS. VENABLE:
I wrote you that my lawyers and bankers and certified public
accountants were setting up the Sebastian Venable Memorial
Foundation to subsidize the work of young people like you
that are pushing out the frontiers of art and science but have
a financial problem. You have a financial problem, don't you,
Doctor?

DOCTOR:
Yes, we do have that problem. My work is such a *new* and
radical thing that people in charge of state funds are naturally
a little scared of it and keep us on a small budget, so small
that—. We need a separate ward for my patients, I need
trained assistants, I'd like to marry a girl I can't afford to
marry!—But there's also the problem of getting right patients,
not just—criminal psychopaths that the State turns over to us
for my operation!—because it's—well—risky. . . . I don't want
to turn you against my work at Lion's View but I have to be
honest with you. There is a good deal of risk in my operation.
Whenever you enter the brain with a foreign object . . .

MRS. VENABLE:
Yes.

29

DOCTOR:
—Even a needle-thin knife ..

MRS. VENABLE:
Yes.

DOCTOR:
—In a skilled surgeon's fingers ...

MRS. VENABLE:
Yes.

DOCTOR:
—There is a good deal of risk involved in—the operation. ...

MRS. VENABLE:
You said that it pacifies them, it quiets them down, it suddenly makes them peaceful.

DOCTOR:
Yes. It does that, that much we already know, but—

MRS. VENABLE:
What?

DOCTOR:
Well, it will be ten years before we can tell if the immediate benefits of the operation will be lasting or—passing or even if there'd still be—and this is what haunts me about it!—any possibility, afterwards, of—reconstructing a—totally sound person, it may be that the person will always be limited afterwards, relieved of acute disturbances but—*limited,* Mrs. Venable. ...

MRS. VENABLE:
Oh, but what a blessing to them, Doctor, to be just peaceful, to be just suddenly—peaceful. ...

[*A bird sings sweetly in the garden.*]

After all that horror, after those nightmares: just to be able

30

to lift up their eyes and see—[*She looks up and raises a hand to indicate the sky*]—a sky not as black with savage, devouring birds as the sky that we saw in the Encantadas, Doctor.

DOCTOR:
—Mrs. Venable? I can't guarantee that a lobotomy would stop her—*babbling*!!

MRS. VENABLE:
That may be, maybe not, but after the operation, who would *believe* her, Doctor?

[*Pause: faint jungle music.*]

DOCTOR [*quietly*]:
My God. [*Pause.*]—Mrs. Venable, suppose after meeting the girl and observing the girl and hearing this story she babbles— I still shouldn't feel that her condition's—intractable enough! to justify the risks of—suppose I shouldn't feel that non-surgical treatment such as insulin shock and electric shock and—

MRS. VENABLE:
SHE'S HAD ALL THAT AT SAINT MARY'S!! Nothing else is left for her.

DOCTOR:
But if I disagreed with you? [*Pause.*]

MRS. VENABLE:
That's just part of a question: finish the question, Doctor.

DOCTOR:
Would you still be interested in my work at Lion's View? I mean would the Sebastian Venable Memorial Foundation still be interested in it?

MRS. VENABLE:
Aren't we always more interested in a thing that concerns us personally, Doctor?

31

DOCTOR:
Mrs. Venable!!

[*Catharine Holly appears between the lace window curtains.*]

You're such an innocent person that it doesn't occur to you, it obviously hasn't even occurred to you that anybody less innocent than you are could possibly interpret this offer of a subsidy as—well, as sort of a *bribe?*

MRS. VENABLE [*laughs, throwing her head back*]:
Name it that—I don't care—. There's just two things to remember. She's a destroyer. My son was a *creator!*—Now if my honesty's shocked you—pick up your little black bag without the subsidy in it, and run away from this garden!—Nobody's heard our conversation but you and I, Doctor Sugar. . . .

[*Miss Foxhill comes out of the house and calls.*]

MISS FOXHILL:
Mrs. Venable?

MRS. VENABLE:
What is it, what do you want, Miss Foxhill?

MISS FOXHILL:
Mrs. Venable? Miss Holly is here, with—

[*Mrs. Venable sees Catharine at the window.*]

MRS. VENABLE:
Oh, my God. There she is, in the window!—I told you I didn't want her to enter my house again, I told you to meet them at the door and lead them around the side of the house to the garden and you didn't listen. I'm not ready to face her. I have to have my five o'clock cocktail first, to fortify me. Take my chair inside. Doctor? Are you still here? I thought you'd run out of the garden. I'm going back through the

32

garden to the other entrance. Doctor? Sugar? You may stay in the garden if you wish to or run out of the garden if you wish to or go in this way if you wish to or do anything that you wish to but I'm going to have my five o'clock daiquiri, *frozen!*—before I face her. . . .

[*All during this she has been sailing very slowly off through the garden like a stately vessel at sea with a fair wind in her sails, a pirate's frigate or a treasure-laden galleon. The young Doctor stares at Catharine framed by the lace window curtains. Sister Felicity appears beside her and draws her away from the window. Music: an ominous fanfare. Sister Felicity holds the door open for Catharine as the Doctor starts quickly forward. He starts to pick up his bag but doesn't. Catharine rushes out, they almost collide with each other.*]

CATHARINE:
Excuse me.

DOCTOR:
I'm sorry. . . .

[*She looks after him as he goes into the house.*]

SISTER FELICITY:
Sit down and be still till your family come outside.

DIM OUT

SCENE TWO

Catharine removes a cigarette from a lacquered box on the table and lights it. The following quick, cadenced lines are accompanied by quick, dancelike movement, almost formal, as the Sister in her sweeping white habit, which should be starched to make a crackling sound, pursues the girl about the white wicker patio table and among the wicker chairs: this can be accompanied by quick music.

SISTER:
What did you take out of that box on the table?

CATHARINE:
Just a cigarette, Sister.

SISTER:
Put it back in the box.

CATHARINE:
Too late, it's already lighted.

SISTER:
Give it here.

CATHARINE:
Oh, please, let me smoke, Sister!

SISTER:
Give it here.

CATHARINE:
Please, Sister Felicity.

SISTER:
Catharine, give it here. You know that you're not allowed to smoke at Saint Mary's.

CATHARINE:
We're not at Saint Mary's, this is an afternoon out.

SISTER:
You're still in my charge. I can't permit you to smoke because the last time you smoked you dropped a lighted cigarette on your dress and started a fire.

CATHARINE:
Oh, I did not start a fire. I just burned a hole in my skirt because I was half unconscious under medication. [*She is now back of a white wicker chair.*]

SISTER [*overlapping her*]:
Catharine, give it here.

CATHARINE:
Don't be such a bully!

SISTER:
Disobedience has to be paid for later.

CATHARINE:
All right, I'll pay for it later.

SISTER [*overlapping*]:
Give me that cigarette or I'll make a report that'll put you

36

right back on the violent ward, if you don't. [*She claps her hands twice and holds one hand out across the table.*]

CATHARINE [*overlapping*]:
I'm not being violent, Sister.

SISTER [*overlapping*]:
Give me that cigarette, I'm holding my hand out for it!

CATHARINE:
All right, take it, here, take it!

[*She thrusts the lighted end of the cigarette into the palm of the Sister's hand. The Sister cries out and sucks her burned hand.*]

SISTER:
You burned me with it!

CATHARINE:
I'm sorry, I didn't mean to.

SISTER [*shocked, hurt*]:
You deliberately burned me!

CATHARINE [*overlapping*]:
You said give it to you and so I gave it to you.

SISTER [*overlapping*]:
You stuck the lighted end of that cigarette in my hand!

CATHARINE [*overlapping*]:
I'm *sick,* I'm *sick!*—of being *bossed* and *bullied*!

SISTER [*commandingly*]:
Sit down!

[*Catharine sits down stiffly in a white wicker chair on fore-stage, facing the audience. The Sister resumes sucking the burned palm of her hand. Ten beats. Then from inside the house the whirr of a mechanical mixer.*]

37

CATHARINE:
There goes the Waring Mixer, Aunt Violet's about to have her five o'clock frozen daiquiri, you could set a watch by it! [*She almost laughs. Then she draws a deep, shuddering breath and leans back in her chair, but her hands remain clenched on the white wicker arms.*]—We're in Sebastian's garden. *My God, I can still cry!*

SISTER:
Did you have any medication before you went out?

CATHARINE:
No. I didn't have any. Will you give me some, Sister?

SISTER [*almost gently*]:
I can't. I wasn't told to. However, I think the doctor will give you something.

CATHARINE:
The young blond man I bumped into?

SISTER:
Yes. The young doctor's a specialist from another hospital.

CATHARINE:
What hospital?

SISTER:
A word to the wise is sufficient. . . .

[*The Doctor has appeared in the window.*]

CATHARINE [*rising abruptly*]:
I knew I was being watched, he's in the window, staring out at me!

SISTER:
Sit down and be still. Your family's coming outside.

CATHARINE [*overlapping*]:
LION'S VIEW, IS IT! DOCTOR?

[*She has advanced toward the bay window. The Doctor draws back, letting the misty white gauze curtains down to obscure him.*]

SISTER [*rising with a restraining gesture which is almost pitying*]:

Sit down, dear.

CATHARINE:

IS IT LION'S VIEW? DOCTOR?!

SISTER:

Be still. . . .

CATHARINE:

WHEN CAN I STOP RUNNING DOWN THAT STEEP WHITE STREET IN CABEZA DE LOBO?

SISTER:

Catharine, dear, sit down.

CATHARINE:

I loved him, Sister! Why wouldn't he let me save him? I tried to hold onto his hand but he struck me away and ran, ran, ran in the wrong direction, Sister!

SISTER:

Catharine, dear—be still.

[*The Sister sneezes.*]

CATHARINE:

Bless you, Sister. [*She says this absently, still watching the window.*]

SISTER:

Thank you.

CATHARINE:

The Doctor's still at the window but he's too blond to hide

39

behind window curtains, he catches the light, he shines through them. [*She turns from the window.*]—We were *going* to blonds, blonds were next on the menu.

SISTER:
Be still now. Quiet, dear.

CATHARINE:
Cousin Sebastian said he was famished for blonds, he was fed up with the dark ones and was famished for blonds. All the travel brochures he picked up were advertisements of the blond northern countries. I think he'd already booked us to— Copenhagen or—Stockholm.—Fed up with dark ones, famished for light ones: that's how he talked about people, as if they were—items on a menu.—"That one's delicious-looking, that one is appetizing," or "that one is *not* appetizing"—I think because he was really nearly half-starved from living on pills and salads. . . .

SISTER:
Stop it!—Catharine, be still.

CATHARINE:
He liked me and so I loved him. . . . [*She cries a little again.*] If he'd kept hold of my hand I could have saved him!—Sebastian suddenly said to me last summer: "Let's fly north, little bird—I want to walk under those radiant, cold northern lights—I've never *seen* the aurora borealis!"—Somebody said once or wrote, once: "We're all of us children in a vast kindergarten trying to spell God's name with the wrong alphabet blocks!"

MRS. HOLLY [*offstage*]:
Sister?

[*The Sister rises.*]

CATHARINE [*rising*]:
I think it's *me* they're calling, they call *me* "Sister," Sister!

40

SCENE THREE

The Sister resumes her seat impassively as the girl's mother and younger brother appear from the garden. The mother, Mrs. Holly, is a fatuous Southern lady who requires no other description. The brother, George, is typically good-looking, he has the best "looks" of the family, tall and elegant of figure. They enter.

MRS. HOLLY:
Catharine, dear! Catharine—

[*They embrace tentatively.*]

Well, well! Doesn't she look fine, George?

GEORGE:
Uh huh.

CATHARINE:
They send you to the beauty parlor whenever you're going to have a family visit. Other times you look awful, you can't

41

have a compact or lipstick or anything made out of metal because they're afraid you'll swallow it.

MRS. HOLLY [*giving a tinkly little laugh*]:
I think she looks just splendid, don't you, George?

GEORGE:
Can't we talk to her without the nun for a minute?

MRS. HOLLY:
Yes, I'm sure it's all right to. Sister?

CATHARINE:
Excuse me, Sister Felicity, this is my mother, Mrs. Holly, and my brother, George.

SISTER:
How do you do.

GEORGE:
How d'ya do.

CATHARINE:
This is Sister Felicity. . . .

MRS. HOLLY:
We're so happy that Catharine's at Saint Mary's! So very grateful for all you're doing for her.

SISTER [*sadly, mechanically*]:
We do the best we can for her, Mrs. Holly.

MRS. HOLLY:
I'm sure you do. Yes, well—I wonder if you would mind if we had a little private chat with our Cathie?

SISTER:
I'm not supposed to let her out of my sight.

MRS. HOLLY:
It's just for a minute. You can sit in the hall or the garden

and we'll call you right back here the minute the private part of the little talk is over.

[*Sister Felicity withdraws with an uncertain nod and a swish of starched fabric.*]

GEORGE [*to Catharine*]:
Jesus! What are you up to? Huh? Sister? Are you trying to RUIN us?!

MRS. HOLLY:
GAWGE! WILL YOU BE QUIET. You're upsetting your sister!

[*He jumps up and stalks off a little, rapping his knee with his zipper-covered tennis racket.*]

CATHARINE:
How elegant George looks.

MRS. HOLLY:
George inherited Cousin Sebastian's wardrobe but everything else is in probate! Did you know that? That everything else is in probate and Violet can keep it in probate just as long as she wants to?

CATHARINE:
Where is Aunt Violet?

MRS. HOLLY:
George, come back here!

[*He does, sulkily.*]

Violet's on her way down.

GEORGE:
Yeah. Aunt Violet has an elevator now.

MRS. HOLLY:
Yais, she has, she's had an elevator installed where the back

, stairs were, and, Sister, it's the cutest little thing you ever did see! It's paneled in Chinese lacquer, black an' gold Chinese lacquer, with lovely bird-pictures on it. But there's only room for two people at a time in it. George and I came down on foot.—I think she's havin' her frozen daiquiri now, she still has a frozen daiquiri promptly at five o'clock ev'ry afternoon in the world . . . in warm weather. . . . Sister, the horrible death of Sebastian just about *killed* her!—She's now slightly better . . . but it's a question of time.—Dear, you know, I'm sure that you understand, why we haven't been out to see you at Saint Mary's. They said you were too disturbed, and a family visit might disturb you more. But I want you to know that nobody, absolutely nobody in the city, knows a thing about what you've been through. Have they, George? Not a thing. Not a soul even knows that you've come back from Europe. When people enquire, when they question us about you, we just say that you've stayed abroad to study something or other. [*She catches her breath.*] Now. Sister?—I want you to please be *very* careful what you say to your Aunt Violet about what happened to Sebastian in Cabeza de Lobo.

CATHARINE:

What do you want me to say about what—?

MRS. HOLLY:

Just don't repeat that same fantastic story! For my sake and George's sake, the sake of your brother and mother, don't repeat that horrible story again! Not to Violet! Will you?

CATHARINE:

Then I am going to have to tell Aunt Violet what happened to her son in Cabeza de Lobo?

MRS. HOLLY:

Honey, that's why you're here. She has *INSISTED* on hearing it straight from YOU!

44

GEORGE:

You were the only witness to it, Cathie.

CATHARINE:

No, there were others. That *ran*.

MRS. HOLLY:

Oh, Sister, you've just had a little sort of a—*nightmare* about it! Now, listen to me, will you, Sister? Sebastian has left, has BEQUEATHED!—to you an' Gawge in his *will*—

GEORGE [*religiously*]:

To each of us, fifty grand, each!—AFTER! TAXES!—GET IT?

CATHARINE:

Oh, yes, but if they give me an injection—I won't have any choice but to tell exactly what happened in Cabeza de Lobo last summer. Don't you see? I won't have any choice but to tell the truth. It makes you tell the truth because it shuts something off that might make you able not to and *everything* comes out, decent or *not* decent, you have no control, but always, always the truth!

MRS. HOLLY:

Catharine, darling. I don't know the full story, but surely you're not too sick in your *head* to know in your *heart* that the story you've been telling is just—too—

GEORGE [*cutting in*]:

Cathie, Cathie, you got to forget that story! Can'tcha? For *your* fifty grand?

MRS. HOLLY:

Because if Aunt Vi contests the will, and we know she'll contest it, she'll keep it in the courts forever!—We'll be—

GEORGE:

It's in PROBATE NOW! And'll never get out of probate

45

until you drop that story—we can't afford to hire lawyers good enough to contest it! So if you don't stop telling that crazy story, we won't have a pot to—cook *greens* in!

[*He turns away with a fierce grimace and a sharp, abrupt wave of his hand, as if slapping down something. Catharine stares at his tall back for a moment and laughs wildly.*]

MRS. HOLLY:
Catharine, don't laugh like that, it scares me, Catharine.

[*Jungle birds scream in the garden.*]

GEORGE [*turning his back on his sister*]:
Cathie, the money is all tied up.

[*He stoops over sofa, hands on flannel knees, speaking directly into Catharine's face as if she were hard of hearing. She raises a hand to touch his cheek affectionately; he seizes the hand and removes it but holds it tight.*]

If Aunt Vi decided to contest Sebastian's will that leaves us all of this cash?!—Am I coming through to you?

CATHARINE:
Yes, little brother, you are.

GEORGE:
You see, Mama, she's crazy like a coyote!

[*He gives her a quick cold kiss*]

We won't get a single damn penny, honest t' God we won't! So you've just GOT to stop tellin' that story about what you say happened to Cousin Sebastian in Cabeza de Lobo, even if it's what it *couldn't* be, TRUE!—You got to drop it, Sister, you can't tell such a story to civilized people in a civilized up-to-date country!

MRS. HOLLY:
Cathie, why, why, why!—did you invent such a tale?

46

CATHARINE:

But, Mother, I DIDN'T invent it. I know it's a hideous story but it's a true story of our time and the world we live in and what did truly happen to Cousin Sebastian in Cabeza de Lobo. . . .

GEORGE:

Oh, then you are going to tell it. Mama, she IS going to tell it! Right to Aunt Vi, and lose us a hundred thousand! —Cathie? You are a BITCH!

MRS. HOLLY:

GAWGE!

GEORGE:

I repeat it, a bitch! She isn't crazy, Mama, she's no more crazy than I am, she's just, just—PERVERSE! Was ALWAYS!— perverse. . . .

[*Catharine turns away and breaks into quiet sobbing.*]

MRS. HOLLY:

Gawge, Gawge, apologize to Sister, this is no way for you to talk to your sister. You come right back over here and tell your sweet little sister you're sorry you spoke like that to her!

GEORGE [*turning back to Catharine*]:

I'm sorry, Cathie, but you know we NEED that money! Mama and me, we—Cathie? I got *ambitions*! And, Cathie, I'm YOUNG!—I *want* things, I *need* them, Cathie! So will you please think about ME? Us?

MISS FOXHILL [*offstage*]:
Mrs. Holly? Mrs. Holly?

MRS. HOLLY:

Somebody's callin' fo' me. Catharine, Gawge put it very badly but you know that it's TRUE! WE DO HAVE TO GET

47

WHAT SEBASTIAN HAS LEFT US IN HIS WILL, DEAR-
EST! AND YOU WON'T LET US DOWN? PROMISE?
YOU WON'T? LET US DOWN?

GEORGE [*fiercely shouting*]: HERE COMES AUNT VI!
Mama, Cathie, Aunt Violet's—here is Aunt Vi!

SCENE FOUR

Mrs. Venable enters downstage area. Entrance music.

MRS. HOLLY:
Cathie! Here's Aunt Vi!

MRS. VENABLE:
She sees me and I see her. That's all that's necessary. Miss
Foxhill, put my chair in this corner. Crank the back up a
little.

[*Miss Foxhill does this business.*]

More. More. Not that much!—Let it back down a little. All
right. Now, then. I'll have my frozen daiquiri, now. . . . Do
any of you want coffee?

GEORGE:
I'd like a chocolate malt.

MRS. HOLLY:
Gawge!

MRS. VENABLE:
This isn't a drugstore.

MRS. HOLLY:
Oh, Gawge is just being Gawge.

MRS. VENABLE:
That's what I *thought* he was being!

[*An uncomfortable silence falls. Miss Foxhill creeps out like a burglar. She speaks in a breathless whisper, presenting a cardboard folder toward Mrs. Venable.*]

MISS FOXHILL:
Here's the portfolio marked Cabeza de Lobo. It has all your correspondence with the police there and the American consul.

MRS. VENABLE:
I asked for the *English transcript*! It's in a separate—

MISS FOXHILL:
Separate, yes, here it is!

MRS. VENABLE:
Oh . . .

MISS FOXHILL:
And here's the report of the private investigators and here's the report of—

MRS. VENABLE:
Yes, yes, yes! Where's the doctor?

MISS FOXHILL:
On the phone in the library!

MRS. VENABLE:
Why does he choose such a moment to make a phone-call?

MISS FOXHILL:
He didn't make a phone-call, he received a phone-call from—

MRS. VENABLE:

Miss Foxhill, why are you talking to me like a burglar!?

[*Miss Foxhill giggles a little desperately.*]

CATHARINE:

Aunt Violet, she's frightened.—Can I move? Can I get up and move around till it starts?

MRS. HOLLY:

Cathie, Cathie, dear, did Gawge tell you that he received bids from every good fraternity on the Tulane campus and went Phi Delt because Paul Junior did?

MRS. VENABLE:

I see that he had the natural tact and good taste to come here this afternoon outfitted from head to foot in clothes that belonged to my son!

GEORGE:

You gave 'em to me, Aunt Vi.

MRS. VENABLE:

I didn't know you'd parade them in front of me, George.

MRS. HOLLY [*quickly*]:

Gawge, tell Aunt Violet how grateful you are for—

GEORGE:

I found a little Jew tailor on Britannia Street that makes alterations so good you'd never guess that they weren't cut *out* for me to *begin* with!

MRS. HOLLY:

AND so reasonable!—Luckily, since it seems that Sebastian's wonderful, wonderful bequest to Gawge an' Cathie is going to be tied up a while!?

GEORGE:

Aunt Vi? About the will?

51

[*Mrs. Holly coughs.*]

I was just wondering if we can't figure out some way to, to—

MRS. HOLLY:
Gawge means to EXPEDITE it! To get through the red tape quicker?

MRS. VENABLE:
I understand his meaning. Foxhill, get the Doctor.

[*She has risen with her cane and hobbled to the door.*]

MISS FOXHILL [*exits calling*]:
Doctor!

MRS. HOLLY:
Gawge, no more about money.

GEORGE:
How do we know we'll ever see her again?

[*Catharine gasps and rises; she moves downstage, followed quickly by Sister Felicity.*]

SISTER [*mechanically*]:
What's wrong, dear?

CATHARINE:
I think I'm just dreaming this, it doesn't seem real!

[*Miss Foxhill comes back out, saying:*]

FOXHILL:
He had to answer an urgent call from Lion's View.

[*Slight, tense pause.*]

MRS. HOLLY:
Violet! *Not* Lion's View!

[*Sister Felicity had started conducting Catharine back to the patio; she stops her, now.*]

SISTER:
Wait, dear.

CATHARINE:
What for? I know what's coming.

MRS. VENABLE [*at same time*]:
Why? are you all prepared to put out a thousand a month plus extra charges for treatments to keep the girl at St. Mary's?

MRS. HOLLY:
Cathie? Cathie, dear?

[*Catharine has returned with the Sister.*]

Tell Aunt Violet how grateful you are for her makin' it possible for you to rest an' recuperate at such a sweet, sweet place as St. Mary's!

CATHARINE:
No place for lunatics is a sweet, sweet place.

MRS. HOLLY:
But the food's good there. Isn't the food good there?

CATHARINE:
Just give me written permission not to eat fried grits. I had yard privileges till I refused to eat fried grits.

SISTER:
She lost yard privileges because she couldn't be trusted in the yard without constant supervision or even with it because she'd run to the fence and make signs to cars on the highway.

CATHARINE:
Yes, I did, I did that because I've been trying for weeks to get a message out of that "sweet, sweet place."

MRS. HOLLY:
What message, dear?

53

CATHARINE:
I got panicky, Mother.

MRS. HOLLY:
Sister, I don't understand.

GEORGE:
What're you scared of, Sister?

CATHARINE:
What they might do to me now, after they've done all the rest!—That man in the window's a specialist from Lion's View! We get newspapers. I know what they're . . .

[*The Doctor comes out.*]

MRS. VENABLE:
Why, Doctor, I thought you'd left us with just that little black bag to remember you by!

DOCTOR:
Oh, no. Don't you remember our talk? I had to answer a call about a patient that—

MRS. VENABLE:
This is Dr. Cukrowicz. He says it means "sugar" and we can call him "Sugar"—

[*George laughs.*]

He's a specialist from Lion's View.

CATHARINE [*cutting in*]:
WHAT DOES HE SPECIALIZE IN?

MRS. VENABLE:
Something new. When other treatments have failed.

[*Pause. The jungle clamor comes up and subsides again.*]

CATHARINE:
Do you want to bore a hole in my skull and turn a knife in my brain? Everything else was done to me!

54

[*Mrs. Holly sobs. George raps his knee with the tennis racket.*]

You'd have to have my mother's permission for that.

MRS. VENABLE:
I'm paying to keep you in a private asylum.

CATHARINE:
You're not my legal guardian.

MRS. VENABLE:
Your mother's dependent on me. All of you are!—Financially. . . .

CATHARINE:
I think the situation is—clear to me, now. . . .

MRS. VENABLE:
Good! In that case. . . .

DOCTOR:
I think a quiet atmosphere will get us the best results.

MRS. VENABLE:
I don't know what you mean by a quiet atmosphere. She shouted, I didn't.

DOCTOR:
Mrs. Venable, let's try to keep things on a quiet level, now. Your niece seems to be disturbed.

MRS. VENABLE:
She has every reason to be. She took my son from me, and then she—

CATHARINE:
Aunt Violet, you're not being fair.

MRS. VENABLE:
Oh, aren't I?

55

CATHARINE [*to the others*]:
She's not being fair.

[*Then back to Mrs. Venable:*]

Aunt Violet, you know why Sebastian asked me to travel with him.

MRS. VENABLE:
Yes, I *do* know why!

CATHARINE:
You weren't able to travel. You'd had a—[*She stops short.*]

MRS. VENABLE:
Go on! *What* had I had? Are you afraid to say it in front of the Doctor? She meant that I had a stroke.—I DID NOT HAVE A STROKE!—I had a slight aneurism. You know what that is, Doctor? A little vascular convulsion! Not a hemorrhage, just a little convulsion of a blood-vessel. I had it when I discovered that she was trying to take my son away from me. Then I had it. It gave a little temporary—muscular —contraction.—To one side of my face. . . . [*She crosses back into main acting area.*] These people are not blood-relatives of mine, they're my dead husband's relations. I always detested these people, my dead husband's sister and—her two worthless children. But I did more than my duty to keep their heads above water. To please my son, whose weakness was being excessively softhearted, I went to the expense and humili-ation, yes, public humiliation, of giving this girl a debut which was a fiasco. Nobody liked her when I brought her out. Oh, she had some kind of—notoriety! She had a sharp tongue that some people mistook for wit. A habit of laughing in the faces of decent people which would infuriate them, and also re-flected adversely on me and Sebastian, too. But, he, Sebastian, was amused by this girl. While I was disgusted, sickened. And halfway through the season, she was dropped off the

56

party lists, yes, dropped off the lists in spite of my position. Why? Because she'd lost her head over a young married man, made a scandalous scene at a Mardi Gras ball, in the middle of the ballroom. Then everybody dropped her like a hot—rock, but—[*She loses her breath.*] My son, Sebastian, still felt sorry for her and took her with him last summer instead of me. . . .

CATHARINE [*springing up with a cry*]:
I can't change truth, I'm not God! I'm not even sure that He could, I don't think God can change truth! How can I change the story of what happened to her son in Cabeza de Lobo?

MRS. VENABLE [*at the same time*]:
She was in love with my son!

CATHARINE [*overlapping*]:
Let me go back to Saint Mary's. Sister Felicity, let's go back to Saint—

MRS. VENABLE [*overlapping*]:
Oh, no! That's not where you'll go!

CATHARINE [*overlapping*]:
All right, *Lion's View* but don't ask me to—

MRS. VENABLE [*overlapping*]:
You *know* that you were!

CATHARINE [*overlapping*]:
That I was *what,* Aunt Violet?

MRS. VENABLE [*overlapping*]:
Don't call me "Aunt," you're the niece of my dead husband, not me!

MRS. HOLLY [*overlapping*]:
Catharine, Catharine, don't upset your—Doctor? Oh, Doctor!

[*But the Doctor is calmly observing the scene, with detach-*

ment. The jungle garden is loud with the sounds of its feathered and scaled inhabitants.]

CATHARINE:
I don't want to, I didn't want to come here! I know what she thinks, she thinks I murdered her son, she thinks that I was responsible for his death.

MRS. VENABLE:
That's right. I told him when he told me that he was going with you in my place last summer that I'd never see him again and I never did. And only you know why!

CATHARINE:
Oh, my God, I—

[*She rushes out toward garden, followed immediately by the Sister.*]

SISTER:
Miss Catharine, Miss Catharine—

DOCTOR [*overlapping*]:
Mrs. Venable?

SISTER [*overlapping*]:
Miss Catharine?

DOCTOR [*overlapping*]:
Mrs. Venable?

MRS. VENABLE:
What?

DOCTOR:
I'd like to be left alone with Miss Catharine for a few minutes.

MRS. HOLLY:
George, talk to her, George.

[*George crouches appealingly before the old lady's chair, peering close into her face, a hand on her knee.*]

58

GEORGE:

Aunt Vi? Cathie can't go to Lion's View. Everyone in the Garden District would know you'd put your niece in a state asylum, Aunt Vi.

MRS. VENABLE:

Foxhill!

GEORGE:

What do you want, Aunt Vi?

MRS. VENABLE:

Let go of my chair. Foxhill? Get me away from these people!

GEORGE:

Aunt Vi, listen, think of the talk it—

MRS. VENABLE:

I can't get up! Push me, push me away!

GEORGE [*rising but holding chair*]:

I'll push her, Miss Foxhill.

MRS. VENABLE:

Let go of my chair or—

MISS FOXHILL:

Mr. Holly, I—

GEORGE:

I got to talk to her.

[*He pushes her chair downstage.*]

MRS. VENABLE:

Foxhill!

MISS FOXHILL:

Mr. Holly, she doesn't want you to push her.

GEORGE:

I know what I'm doing, leave me alone with Aunt Vi!

59

MRS. VENABLE:
Let go me or I'll *strike* you!

GEORGE:
Oh, Aunt Vi!

MRS. VENABLE:
Foxhill!

MRS. HOLLY:
George—

GEORGE:
Aunt Vi?

[*She strikes at him with her cane. He releases the chair and Miss Foxhill pushes her off. He trots after her a few steps, then he returns to Mrs. Holly, who is sobbing into a handkerchief. He sighs, and sits down beside her, taking her hand. The scene fades as light is brought up on Catharine and the Sister in the garden. The Doctor comes up to them. Mrs. Holly stretches her arms out to George, sobbing, and he crouches before her chair and rests his head in her lap. She strokes his head. During this: the Sister has stood beside Catharine, holding onto her arm.*]

CATHARINE:
You don't have to hold onto me. I can't run away.

DOCTOR:
Miss Catharine?

CATHARINE:
What?

DOCTOR:
Your aunt is a very sick woman. She had a stroke last spring?

CATHARINE:
Yes, she did, but she'll never admit it. . . .

60

DOCTOR:

You have to understand why.

CATHARINE:

I do, I understand why. I didn't want to come here.

DOCTOR:

Miss Catharine, do you hate her?

CATHARINE:

I don't understand what hate is. How can you hate anybody and still be sane? You see, I still think I'm sane!

DOCTOR:

You think she did have a stroke?

CATHARINE:

She had a slight stroke in April. It just affected one side, the left side, of her face . . . but it was disfiguring, and after that, Sebastian couldn't use her.

DOCTOR:

Use her? Did you say use her?

[*The sounds of the jungle garden are not loud but ominous.*]

CATHARINE:

Yes, we all use each other and that's what we think of as love, and not being able to use each other is what's—*hate.* . . .

DOCTOR:

Do you hate her, Miss Catharine?

CATHARINE:

Didn't you ask me that, once? And didn't I say that I didn't understand hate. A ship struck an iceberg at sea—everyone sinking—

DOCTOR:

Go on, Miss Catharine!

CATHARINE:

But that's no reason for everyone drowning for hating everyone drowning! Is it, Doctor?

DOCTOR:

Tell me: what was your feeling for your cousin Sebastian?

CATHARINE:

He liked me and so I loved him.

DOCTOR:

In what way did you love him?

CATHARINE:

The only way he'd accept:—a sort of motherly way. I tried to save him, Doctor.

DOCTOR:

From what? Save him from what?

CATHARINE:

Completing!—a sort of!—*image*!—he had of himself as a sort of!—*sacrifice* to a!—*terrible* sort of a—

DOCTOR:

—God?

CATHARINE:

Yes, a—*cruel* one, Doctor!

DOCTOR:

How did you feel about that?

CATHARINE:

Doctor, my feelings are the sort of feelings that you have in a dream. . . .

DOCTOR:

Your life doesn't seem real to you?

62

CATHARINE:

Suddenly last winter I began to write my journal in the third person.

[*He grasps her elbow and leads her out upon forestage. At the same time Miss Foxhill wheels Mrs. Venable off, Mrs. Holly weeps into a handkerchief and George rises and shrugs and turns his back to the audience.*]

DOCTOR:

Something happened last winter?

CATHARINE:

At a Mardi Gras ball some—some boy that took me to it got too drunk to stand up! [*A short, mirthless note of laughter.*] I wanted to go home. My coat was in the cloakroom, they couldn't find the check for it in his pockets. I said, "Oh, hell, let it go!"—I started out for a taxi. Somebody took my arm and said, "I'll drive you home." He took off his coat as we left the hotel and put it over my shoulders, and then I looked at him and—I don't think I'd ever even seen him before then, really!—He took me home in his car but took me another place first. We stopped near the Duelling Oaks at the end of Esplanade Street. . . . Stopped!—I said, "What for?"—He didn't answer, just struck a match in the car to light a cigarette in the car and I looked at him in the car and I knew "what for"!—I think I got out of the car before he got out of the car, and we walked through the wet grass to the great misty oaks as if somebody was calling us for help there!

[*Pause. The subdued, toneless bird-cries in the garden turn to a single bird-song.*]

DOCTOR:

After that?

CATHARINE:

I lost him.—He took me home and said an awful thing to

63

me. "We'd better forget it," he said, "my wife's expecting a child and—."—I just entered the house and sat there thinking a little and then I suddenly called a taxi and went right back to the Roosevelt Hotel ballroom. The ball was still going on. I thought I'd gone back to pick up my borrowed coat but that wasn't what I'd gone back for. I'd gone back to make a scene on the floor of the ballroom, yes, I didn't stop at the cloak-room to pick up Aunt Violet's old mink stole, no, I rushed right into the ballroom and spotted him on the floor and ran up to him and beat him as hard as I could in the face and chest with my fists till—Cousin Sebastian took me away.— After that, the next morning, I started writing my diary in the third person, singular, such as "She's still living this morning," meaning that *I* was. . . . —"WHAT'S NEXT FOR HER? GOD KNOWS!"—I couldn't go out any more. —However one morning my Cousin Sebastian came in my bedroom and said: "Get up!"—Well . . . if you're still alive after dying, well then, you're obedient, Doctor.—I got up. He took me downtown to a place for passport photos. Said: "Mother can't go abroad with me this summer. You're going to go with me this summer instead of Mother."—If you don't believe me, read my journal of Paris!—"She woke up at daybreak this morning, had her coffee and dressed and took a brief walk—"

DOCTOR:
Who did?

CATHARINE:
She did. *I* did—from the Hotel Plaza Athénée to the Place de l'Étoile as if pursued by a pack of Siberian wolves! [*She laughs her tired, helpless laugh.*]—Went right through all stop signs—couldn't wait for green signals.—"Where did she think she was going? Back to the Duelling Oaks?"—Everything chilly and dim but his hot, ravenous mouth! on—

64

DOCTOR:

Miss Catharine, let me give you something.

[*The others go out, leaving Catharine and the Doctor onstage.*]

CATHARINE:

Do I have to have the injection again, this time? What am I going to be stuck with this time, Doctor? I don't care. I've been stuck so often that if you connected me with a garden hose I'd make a good sprinkler.

DOCTOR [*preparing needle*]:

Please take off your jacket.

[*She does. The Doctor gives her an injection.*]

CATHARINE:

I didn't feel it.

DOCTOR:

That's good. Now sit down.

[*She sits down.*]

CATHARINE:

Shall I start counting backwards from a hundred?

DOCTOR:

Do you like counting backwards?

CATHARINE:

Love it! Just love it! One hundred! Ninety-nine! Ninety-eight! Ninety-seven. Ninety-six. Ninety—five—. Oh!—I already feel it! How funny!

DOCTOR:

That's right. Close your eyes for a minute.

[*He moves his chair closer to hers. Half a minute passes.*]

Miss Catharine? I want you to give me something.

65

CATHARINE:
Name it and it's yours, Doctor Sugar.

DOCTOR:
Give me all your resistance.

CATHARINE:
Resistance to what?

DOCTOR:
The truth. Which you're going to tell me.

CATHARINE:
The truth's the one thing I have never resisted!

DOCTOR:
Sometimes people just think they don't resist it, but still do.

CATHARINE:
They say it's at the bottom of a bottomless well, you know:

DOCTOR:
Relax.

CATHARINE:
Truth.

DOCTOR:
Don't talk.

CATHARINE:
Where was I, now? At ninety?

DOCTOR:
You don't have to count backwards.

CATHARINE:
At ninety something?

DOCTOR:
You can open your eyes.

CATHARINE:
Oh, I do feel funny!

[*Silence, pause.*]

You know what I think you're doing? I think you're trying to hypnotize me. Aren't you? You're looking so straight at me and doing something to me with your eyes and your—eyes. . . . Is that what you're doing to me?

DOCTOR:
Is that what you *feel* I'm doing?

CATHARINE:
Yes! I feel so peculiar. And it's not just the drug.

DOCTOR:
Give me all your resistance. See. I'm holding my hand out. I want you to put yours in mine and give me all your resistance. Pass all of your resistance out of your hand to mine.

CATHARINE:
Here's my hand. But there's no resistance in it.

DOCTOR:
You are totally passive.

CATHARINE:
Yes, I am.

DOCTOR:
You will do what I ask.

CATHARINE:
Yes, I will try.

DOCTOR:
You will tell the true story.

CATHARINE:
Yes, I will.

DOCTOR:
The absolutely true story. No lies, nothing not spoken. Everything told, exactly.

67

CATHARINE:

Everything. Exactly. Because I'll have to. Can I—can I stand up?

DOCTOR:

Yes, but be careful. You might feel a little bit dizzy.

[*She struggles to rise, then falls back.*]

CATHARINE:

I can't get up! Tell me to. Then I think I could do it.

DOCTOR:

Stand up.

[*She rises unsteadily.*]

CATHARINE:

How funny! Now I can! Oh, I do feel dizzy! Help me, I'm—

[*He rushes to support her.*]

—about to fall over. . . .

[*He holds her. She looks out vaguely toward the brilliant, steaming garden. Looks back at him. Suddenly sways toward him, against him.*]

DOCTOR:

You see, you lost your balance.

CATHARINE:

No, I didn't. I did what I wanted to do without you telling me to.

[*She holds him tight against her.*]

Let me! Let! Let! Let me! Let me, let me, oh, let me. . . .

[*She crushes her mouth to his violently. He tries to disengage himself. She presses her lips to his fiercely, clutching his body against her. Her brother George enters.*]

68

Please hold me! I've been so lonely. It's lonelier than death, if I've gone mad, it's lonelier than death!

GEORGE [*shocked, disgusted*]:
Cathie!—you've got a hell of a nerve.

[*She falls back, panting, covers her face, runs a few paces and grabs the back of a chair. Mrs. Holly enters.*]

MRS. HOLLY:
What's the matter, George? Is Catharine ill?

GEORGE:
No.

DOCTOR:
Miss Catharine had an injection that made her a little unsteady.

MRS. HOLLY:
What did he say about Catharine?

[*Catharine has gone out into the dazzling jungle of the garden.*]

SISTER [*returning*]:
She's gone into the garden.

DOCTOR:
That's all right, she'll come back when I call her.

SISTER:
It may be all right for you. You're not responsible for her.

[*Mrs. Venable has re-entered.*]

MRS. VENABLE:
Call her now!

DOCTOR:
Miss Catharine! Come back.

[*To the Sister:*]

Bring her back, please, Sister!

[*Catharine enters quietly, a little unsteady.*]

Now, Miss Catharine, you're going to tell the true story.

CATHARINE:
Where do I start the story?

DOCTOR:
Wherever you think it started.

CATHARINE:
I think it started the day he was born in this house.

MRS. VENABLE:
Ha! You see!

GEORGE:
Cathie.

DOCTOR:
Let's start later than that. [*Pause.*] Shall we begin with last summer?

CATHARINE:
Oh. Last summer.

DOCTOR:
Yes. Last summer.

[*There is a long pause. The raucous sounds in the garden fade into a bird-song which is clear and sweet. Mrs. Holly coughs. Mrs. Venable stirs impatiently. George crosses downstage to catch Catharine's eye as he lights a cigarette.*]

CATHARINE:
Could I—?

MRS. VENABLE:
Keep that boy away from her!

GEORGE:
She wants to smoke, Aunt Vi.

CATHARINE:
Something helps in the—hands. . . .

SISTER:
Unh unh!

DOCTOR:
It's all right, Sister. [*He lights her cigarette.*] About last summer: how did it begin?

CATHARINE:
It began with his kindness and the six days at sea that took me so far away from the—Duelling Oaks that I forgot them, nearly. He was affectionate with me, so sweet and attentive to me, that some people took us for a honeymoon couple until they noticed that we had—separate staterooms, and—then in Paris, he took me to Patou and Schiaparelli's—*this* is from Schiaparelli's! [*Like a child, she indicates her suit.*]—bought me so many new clothes that I gave away my old ones to make room for my new ones in my new luggage to—travel. . . . I turned into a peacock! Of course, so was *he* one, too. . . .

GEORGE:
Ha Ha!

MRS. VENABLE:
Shh!

CATHARINE:
But then I made the mistake of responding too much to his kindness, of taking hold of his hand before he'd take hold of mine, of holding onto his arm and leaning on his shoulder, of appreciating his kindness more than he wanted me to, and, suddenly, last summer, he began to be restless, and—oh!

DOCTOR:
Go on.

CATHARINE:
The Blue Jay notebook!

DOCTOR:
Did you say notebook?

MRS. VENABLE:
I know what she means by that, she's talking about the school composition book with a Blue Jay trademark that Sebastian used for making notes and revisions on his "Poem of Summer." It went with him everywhere that he went, in his jacket pocket, even his dinner jacket. I have the one that he had with him last summer. *Foxhill! The Blue Jay notebook!*

[*Miss Foxhill rushes in with a gasp.*]

It came with his personal effects shipped back from Cabeza de Lobo.

DOCTOR:
I don't quite get the connection between new clothes and so forth and the Blue Jay notebook.

MRS. VENABLE:
I HAVE IT!—Doctor, tell her I've found it.

[*Miss Foxhill hears this as she comes back out of house: gasps with relief, retires.*]

DOCTOR:
With all these interruptions it's going to be awfully hard to—

MRS. VENABLE:
This is important. I don't know why she mentioned the Blue Jay notebook but I want you to see it. Here it is, here! [*She holds up a notebook and leafs swiftly through the pages.*] Title? "Poem of Summer," and the date of the summer— 1935. After that: *what? Blank pages, blank pages*, nothing but *nothing!*—last summer. . . .

DOCTOR:
What's that got to do with—?

MRS. VENABLE:

His destruction? I'll tell you. A poet's vocation is something that rests on something as thin and fine as the web of a spider, Doctor. That's all that holds him *over*!—out of destruction. . . . Few, very few are able to do it alone! Great help is needed! I *did* give it! She *didn't*.

CATHARINE:

She's right about that. I failed him. I wasn't able to keep the web from—breaking. . . . I saw it breaking but couldn't save or—repair it!

MRS. VENABLE:

There now, the truth's coming out. We had an agreement between us, a sort of contract or covenant between us which he broke last summer when he broke away from me and took her with him, not me! When he was frightened and I knew when and what of, because his hands would shake and his eyes looked in, not out, I'd reach across a table and touch his hands and say not a word, just look, and touch his hands with my hand until his hands stopped shaking and his eyes looked out, not in, and in the morning, the poem would be continued. *Continued until it was finished!*

[*The following ten speeches are said very rapidly, overlapping.*]

CATHARINE:

I—couldn't!

MRS. VENABLE:

Naturally not! He was *mine*! I *knew* how to help him, I *could*! You didn't, you couldn't!

DOCTOR:

These interruptions—

MRS. VENABLE:

I would say "You *will*" and he *would*, I—!

73

CATHARINE:

Yes, you see, I failed him! And so, last summer, we went to Cabeza de Lobo, we flew down there from where he gave up writing his poem last summer....

MRS. VENABLE:

Because he'd broken our—

CATHARINE:

Yes! Yes, something had broken, that string of pearls that old mothers hold their sons by like a—sort of a—sort of— *umbilical* cord, *long—after* . . .

MRS. VENABLE:

She means that I held him back from—

DOCTOR:

Please!

MRS. VENABLE:

Destruction!

CATHARINE:

All I know is that suddenly, last summer, he wasn't young any more, and we went to Cabeza de Lobo, and he suddenly switched from the evenings to the beach. . . .

DOCTOR:

From evenings? To beach?

CATHARINE:

I mean from the evenings to the afternoons and from the fa—fash—

[*Silence*: *Mrs. Holly draws a long, long painful breath. George stirs impatiently.*]

DOCTOR:

Fashionable! Is that the word you—?

74

CATHARINE:
Yes. Suddenly, last summer Cousin Sebastian changed to the afternoons and the beach.

DOCTOR:
What beach?

CATHARINE:
In Cabeza de Lobo there is a beach that's named for Sebastian's name saint, it's known as La Playa San Sebastian, and that's where we started spending all afternoon, every day.

DOCTOR:
What kind of beach was it?

CATHARINE:
It was a big city beach near the harbor.

DOCTOR:
It was a big public beach?

CATHARINE:
Yes, public.

MRS. VENABLE:
It's little statements like that that give her away.

[*The Doctor rises and crosses to Mrs. Venable without breaking his concentration on Catharine.*]

After all I've told you about his fastidiousness, can you accept such a statement?

DOCTOR:
You mustn't interrupt her.

MRS. VENABLE [*overlapping him*]:
That Sebastian would go every day to some dirty free public beach near a harbor? A man that had to go out a mile in a boat to find water fit to swim in?

75

DOCTOR:

Mrs. Venable, no matter what she says you have to let her say it without any more interruptions or this interview will be useless.

MRS. VENABLE:

I won't speak again. I'll keep still, if it kills me.

CATHARINE:

I don't want to go on. . . .

DOCTOR:

Go on with the story. Every afternoon last summer your Cousin Sebastian and you went out to this free public beach?

CATHARINE:

No, it wasn't the free one, the free one was right next to it, there was a fence between the free beach and the one that we went to that charged a small charge of admission.

DOCTOR:

Yes, and what did you do there?

[*He still stands beside Mrs. Venable and the light gradually changes as the girl gets deeper into her story: the light concentrates on Catharine, the other figures sink into shadow.*]

Did anything happen there that disturbed you about it?

CATHARINE:

Yes!

DOCTOR:

What?

CATHARINE:

He bought me a swim-suit I didn't want to wear. I laughed. I said, "I can't wear that, it's a scandal to the jay-birds!"

76

DOCTOR:

What did you mean by that? That the suit was immodest?

CATHARINE:

My God, yes! It was a one-piece suit made of white lisle, the water made it transparent! [*She laughs sadly at the memory of it.*] —I didn't want to swim in it, but he'd grab my hand and drag me into the water, all the way in, and I'd come out looking naked!

DOCTOR:

Why did he do that? Did you understand why?

CATHARINE:

—Yes! To attract!—Attention.

DOCTOR:

He wanted you to attract attention, did he, because he felt you were moody? Lonely? He wanted to shock you out of your depression last summer?

CATHARINE:

Don't you understand? I was PROCURING for him!

[*Mrs. Venable's gasp is like the sound that a great hooked fish might make.*]

She used to do it, *too.*

[*Mrs. Venable cries out.*]

Not consciously! She didn't *know* that she was procuring for him in the smart, the fashionable places they used to go to before last summer! Sebastian was shy with people. She wasn't. Neither was I. We both did the same thing for him, made contacts for him, but she did it in nice places and in decent ways and I had to do it the way that I just told you! —Sebastian was lonely, Doctor, and the empty Blue Jay notebook got bigger and bigger, so big it was big and empty as

77

that big empty blue sea and sky. . . . I knew what I was doing.
I came out in the French Quarter years before I came out in
the Garden District. . . .

MRS. HOLLY:
Oh, Cathie! Sister . . .

DOCTOR:
Hush!

CATHARINE:
And before long, when the weather got warmer and the beach
so crowded, he didn't need me any more for that purpose. The
ones on the free beach began to climb over the fence or swim
around it, bands of homeless young people that lived on the
free beach like scavenger dogs, hungry children. . . . So now
he let me wear a decent dark suit. I'd go to a faraway empty
end of the beach, write postcards and letters and keep up my—
third-person journal till it was—five o'clock and time to meet
him outside the bathhouses, on the street. . . . He would come
out, *followed.*

DOCTOR:
Who would follow him out?

CATHARINE:
The homeless, hungry young people that had climbed over
the fence from the free beach that they lived on. He'd pass out
tips among them as if they'd all—shined his shoes or called
taxis for him. . . . Each day the crowd was bigger, noisier,
greedier!—Sebastian began to be frightened.—At last we
stopped going out there. . . .

DOCTOR:
And then? After that? After you quit going out to the public
beach?

CATHARINE:
Then one day, a few days after we stopped going out to the

beach—it was one of those white blazing days in Cabeza de Lobo, not a blazing hot *blue* one but a blazing hot *white* one.

DOCTOR:
Yes?

CATHARINE:
We had a late lunch at one of those open-air restaurants on the sea there.—Sebastian was white as the weather. He had on a spotless white silk Shantung suit and a white silk tie and a white panama and white shoes, white—white lizard skin— pumps! He—[*She throws back her head in a startled laugh at the recollection*]—kept touching his face and his throat here and there with a white silk handkerchief and popping little white pills in his mouth, and I knew he was having a bad time with his heart and was frightened about it and that was the reason we hadn't gone out to the beach. . . .

[*During the monologue the lights have changed, the surrounding area has dimmed out and a hot white spot is focused on Catharine.*]

"I think we ought to go north," he kept saying, "I think we've done Cabeza de Lobo, I think we've done it, don't you?" *I* thought we'd done it!—but I had learned it was better not to seem to have an opinion because if I did, well, Sebastian, well, you know Sebastian, he always preferred to do what no one else wanted to do, and I always tried to give the impression that I was agreeing reluctantly to his wishes . . . it was a—game. . . .

SISTER:
She's dropped her cigarette.

DOCTOR:
I've got it, Sister.

[*There are whispers, various movements in the penumbra. The Doctor fills a glass for her from the cocktail shaker.*]

CATHARINE:

Where was I? Oh, yes, that five o'clock lunch at one of those fish-places along the harbor of Cabeza de Lobo, it was between the city and the sea, and there were naked children along the beach which was fenced off with barbed wire from the restaurant and we had our table less than a yard from the barbed wire fence that held the beggars at bay.... There were naked children along the beach, a band of frightfully thin and dark naked children that looked like a flock of plucked birds, and they would come darting up to the barbed wire fence as if blown there by the wind, the hot white wind from the sea, all crying out, "*Pan, pan, pan!*"

DOCTOR [*quietly*]:
What's *pan*?

CATHARINE:

The word for bread, and they made gobbling noises with their little black mouths, stuffing their little black fists to their mouths and making those gobbling noises, with frightful grins!—Of course we were sorry that we had come to this place but it was too late to go....

DOCTOR [*quietly*]:
Why was it "too late to go"?

CATHARINE:

I told you Cousin Sebastian wasn't well. He was popping those little white pills in his mouth. I think he had popped in so many of them that they had made him feel weak.... His, his!—eyes looked—dazed, but he said: "Don't look at those little monsters. Beggars are a social disease in this country. If you look at them, you get sick of the country, it spoils the whole country for you...."

DOCTOR:
Go on.

80

CATHARINE:
I'm going on. I have to wait now and then till it gets clearer.
Under the drug it has to be a vision, or nothing comes. . . .

DOCTOR:
All right?

CATHARINE:
Always when I was with him I did what he told me. I didn't
look at the band of naked children, not even when the waiters
drove them away from the barbed wire fence with sticks!—
Rushing out through a wicket gate like an assault party in
war!—and beating them screaming away from the barbed
wire fence with the sticks. . . . Then! [*Pause.*]

DOCTOR:
Go on, Miss Catherine, what comes next in the vision?

CATHARINE:
The, the the!—band of children began to—serenade us. . . .

DOCTOR:
Do what?

CATHARINE:
Play for us! On instruments! Make music!—if you could call
it music. . . .

DOCTOR:
Oh?

CATHARINE:
Their, their—instruments were—instruments of percussion!—
Do you know what I mean?

DOCTOR [*making a note*]:
Yes. Instruments of percussion such as—*drums?*

CATHARINE:
I stole glances at them when Cousin Sebastian wasn't looking,

81

and as well as I could make out in the white blaze of the sand-beach, the instruments were tin cans strung together.

DOCTOR [*slowly, writing*]:
Tin—cans—strung—together.

CATHARINE:
And, and, and, and—and!—bits of metal, other bits of metal that had been flattened out, made into—

DOCTOR:
What?

CATHARINE:
Cymbals! You know? *Cymbals?*

DOCTOR:
Yes. Brass plates hit together.

CATHARINE:
That's right, Doctor.—Tin cans flattened out and clashed together!—Cymbals. . . .

DOCTOR:
Yes. I understand. What's after that, in the vision?

CATHARINE [*rapidly, panting a little*]:
And others had paper bags, bags made out of—coarse paper! —with something on a string inside the bags which they pulled up and down, back and forth, to make a sort of a—

DOCTOR:
Sort of a—?

CATHARINE:
Noise like—

DOCTOR:
Noise like?

CATHARINE [*rising stiffly from chair*]:
Ooompa! Oompa! Oooooompa!

DOCTOR:
Ahhh . . . a sound like a *tuba*?

CATHARINE:
That's right!—they made a sound like a tuba. . . .

DOCTOR:
Oompa, oompa, oompa, like a tuba.

[*He is making a note of the description.*]

CATHARINE:
Oompa, oompa, oompa, like a—

[*Short pause.*]

DOCTOR:
—Tuba. . . .

CATHARINE:
All during lunch they stayed at a—a fairly *close—distance.*...

DOCTOR:
Go on with the vision, Miss Catharine.

CATHARINE [*striding about the table*]:
Oh, I'm going on, nothing could stop it now!!

DOCTOR:
Your Cousin Sebastian was *entertained* by this—*concert*?

CATHARINE:
I think he was *terrified* of it!

DOCTOR:
Why was he terrified of it?

CATHARINE:
I think he recognized some of the musicians, some of the boys,
between childhood and—older. . . .

DOCTOR:
What did he do? Did he do anything about it, Miss Catharine?
—Did he complain to the manager about it?

CATHARINE:

What manager? *God*? Oh, *no*!—The manager of the fish-place on the beach? Haha!—No!—You don't understand my cousin!

DOCTOR:

What do you mean?

CATHARINE:

He! —*accepted!* —*all!* —as—how!—things!—are!—And thought nobody had any right to complain or interfere in any way whatsoever, and even though he knew that what was awful was awful, that what was wrong was wrong, and my Cousin Sebastian was certainly never sure that anything was wrong!—He thought it unfitting to ever take any action about anything whatsoever!—except to go on doing as something in him directed. . . .

DOCTOR:

What did something in him direct him to do?—I mean on this occasion in Cabeza de Lobo.

CATHARINE:

After the salad, before they brought the coffee, he suddenly pushed himself away from the table, and said, "They've got to stop that! Waiter, make them stop that. I'm not a well man, I have a heart condition, it's making me sick!"—This was the first time that Cousin Sebastian had ever attempted to correct a human situation!—I think perhaps that *that* was his—fatal error. . . . It was then that the waiters, all eight or ten of them, charged out of the barbed wire wicket gate and beat the little musicians away with clubs and skillets and anything hard that they could snatch from the kitchen!—Cousin Sebastian left the table. He stalked out of the restaurant after throwing a handful of paper money on the table and he fled from the place. I followed. It was all white outside. White hot, a blazing white hot, hot blazing white, at five o'clock in the afternoon in the city of—Cabeza de Lobo. It looked as if—

DOCTOR:
It looked as if?

CATHARINE:
As if a huge white bone had caught on fire in the sky and blazed so bright it was white and turned the sky and everything under the sky white with it!

DOCTOR:
—White . . .

CATHARINE:
Yes—white . . .

DOCTOR:
You followed your Cousin Sebastian out of the restaurant onto the hot white street?

CATHARINE:
Running up and down hill. . . .

DOCTOR:
You ran up and down hill?

CATHARINE:
No, no! *Didn't*!—move either *way*!—at first, we were—

[*During this recitation there are various sound effects. The percussive sounds described are very softly employed.*]

I rarely made any suggestion but *this* time I *did*. . . .

DOCTOR:
What did you suggest?

CATHARINE:
Cousin Sebastian seemed to be paralyzed near the entrance of the café, so I said, "Let's go." I remember that it was a very wide and steep white street, and I said, "Cousin Sebastian,

85

down that way is the waterfront and we are more likely to find a taxi near there. . . . Or why don't we go back in?—and have them *call* us a taxi! Oh, let's do! Let's do *that,* that's better!" And he said, "*Mad,* are you *mad*? Go back in that filthy place? Never! That gang of kids shouted vile things about me to the waiters!" "Oh," I said, "then let's go down toward the docks, down there at the bottom of the hill, let's not try to climb the hill in this dreadful heat." And Cousin Sebastian shouted, "Please shut up, let me handle this situation, will you? I want to handle this thing." And he started up the steep street with a hand stuck in his jacket where I knew he was having a pain in his chest from his palpitations. . . . But he walked faster and faster, in panic, but the faster he walked the louder and closer it got!

DOCTOR:
What got louder?

CATHARINE:
The music.

DOCTOR:
The music again.

CATHARINE:
The oompa-oompa of the—following band.—They'd somehow gotten through the barbed wire and out on the street, and they were following, following!—up the blazing white street. The band of naked children pursued us up the steep white street in the sun that was like a great white bone of a giant beast that had caught on fire in the sky!—Sebastian started to run and they all screamed at once and seemed to fly in the air, they outran him so quickly. I screamed. I heard Sebastian scream, he screamed just once before this flock of black plucked little birds that pursued him and overtook him halfway up the white hill.

DOCTOR:

And you, Miss Catharine, what did *you* do, then?

CATHARINE:

Ran!

DOCTOR:

Ran where?

CATHARINE:

Down! Oh, I ran down, the easier direction to run was down, down, down, down!—The hot, white, blazing street, screaming out "Help" all the way, till—

DOCTOR:

What?

CATHARINE:

—Waiters, police, and others—ran out of buildings and rushed back up the hill with me. When we got back to where my Cousin Sebastian had disappeared in the flock of featherless little black sparrows, he—he was lying naked as they had been naked against a white wall, and this you won't believe, nobody *has* believed it, nobody *could* believe it, nobody, nobody on earth could possibly believe it, and I don't *blame* them!—They had *devoured* parts of him.

[*Mrs. Venable cries out softly.*]

Torn or cut parts of him away with their hands or knives or maybe those jagged tin cans they made music with, they had torn bits of him away and stuffed them into those gobbling fierce little empty black mouths of theirs. There wasn't a sound any more, there was nothing to see but Sebastian, what was left of him, that looked like a big white-paper-wrapped bunch of red roses had been *torn, thrown, crushed!*—against that blazing white wall. . . .

[*Mrs. Venable springs with amazing power from her wheel-*

87

chair, stumbles erratically but swiftly toward the girl and tries to strike her with her cane. The Doctor snatches it from her and catches her as she is about to fall. She gasps hoarsely several times as he leads her toward the exit.]

MRS. VENABLE [*offstage*]:
Lion's View! State asylum, cut this hideous story out of her brain!

[*Mrs. Holly sobs and crosses to George, who turns away from her, saying*:]

GEORGE:
Mom, I'll quit school, I'll get a job, I'll—

MRS. HOLLY:
Hush son! Doctor, can't you say something?

[*Pause. The Doctor comes downstage. Catharine wanders out into the garden followed by the Sister.*]

DOCTOR [*after a while, reflectively, into space*]:
I think we ought at least to consider the possibility that the girl's story could be true. . . .

THE END